Calculator Fun

Ruth Merttens
Senior Lecturer, Maths Education, Polytechnic of North London

Tim Rowland
Lecturer in Mathematics, Homerton College, Cambridge

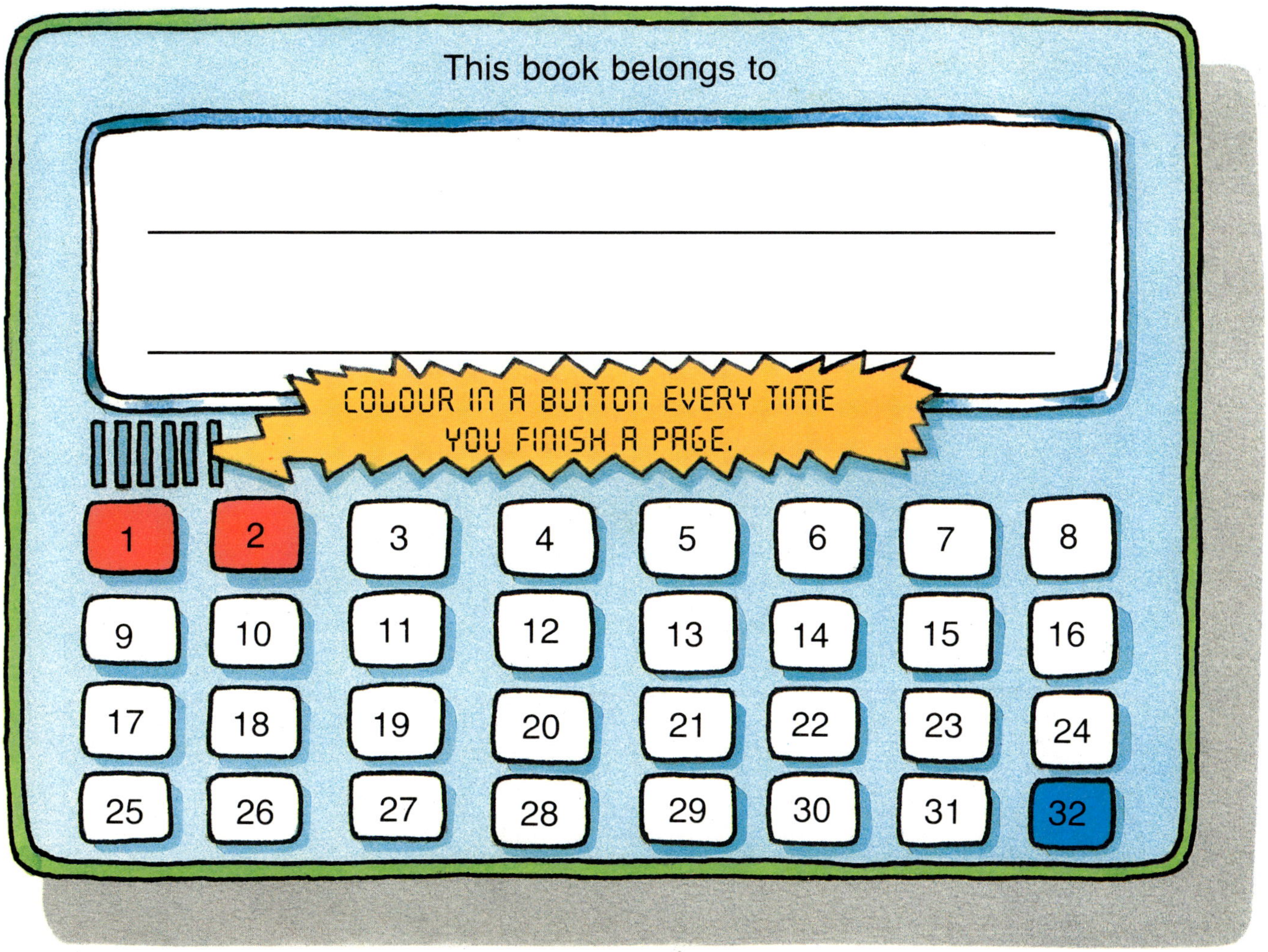

This book belongs to

_____

COLOUR IN A BUTTON EVERY TIME YOU FINISH A PAGE.

1	2	3	4	5	6	7	8
9	10	11	12	13	14	15	16
17	18	19	20	21	22	23	24
25	26	27	28	29	30	31	32

Illustrated by Alan Snow

To Parents

How parents can help

As parents, we can encourage our children's progress in maths by sharing learning activities with them at home. This does not just involve helping them when they are practising skills or trying to remember number facts. It also means joining in as they work out a problem and sharing that moment when things fall into place and are understood.

It is important nowadays that children develop the ability to think logically and creatively in maths. They can no longer progress in secondary school by learning their maths parrot-fashion — the content of the new GCSE exams as well as the demands of employers and higher education, require children to understand what they are doing.

Calculators

Calculators have been used in primary schools for over a decade. Most teachers now accept the positive value of calculators and many use them with children from the age of 6 or 7, as an important resource in the learning of number skills and concepts.

Calculators provide a great means of experimenting and discovery in maths, as well as giving children another way of practising routine number skills, such as tables. In this book there are activities that will enable your child to use the mathematical knowledge he or she already has and to find out fascinating things about numbers and how they work.

Do not be tempted to think that a calculator makes maths easier for children or that it is a substitute for learning. Unless the child understands very well what has to be done to solve a particular mathematical problem, a calculator is useless. Also, calculators enable children — as they do adults — to solve much more difficult and complicated mathematical problems than they would otherwise be able to attempt.

How to use this book

The activities are for you and your child to share. In those that ask the child to investigate something or to find a pattern, it is very helpful if both the 'work' and the discovery are shared. There is much enjoyment in a joint struggle and often greater pleasure in the results. Also, children are less likely to 'give up' under these circumstances. Learning to persevere is very hard for some children but it is well worth the effort in the end.

Don't try to rush or make your child do too much at once. Some activities are quite difficult — you may need to spend a number of sessions on them.

Encourage your child to explain things to you. Putting ideas into words helps children reach a clearer understanding of them.

There is a pull-out **games board** in the centre of this book; games provide a particularly valuable way of helping children to practise skills or to reinforce new concepts.

These activities have been tried and enjoyed by many children and parents, both in schools across the country and in homes as a part of the IMPACT Project (which involves parents in their children's maths).

There is no more effective way of helping your child enjoy maths than by being seen to do so yourself — so join in and enjoy it!

Ruth Merttens

Tim Rowland.

Play with your calculator

You can have good fun just playing with your calculator to find out what it can do. Don't worry if strange things happen when you press some of the keys. It does not matter if you cannot always understand what the calculator is doing. Cat has some ideas to start you off.

Note to Parents

Your child can use **any** calculator, the **simpler** the better (scientific calculators may be confusing at this age). Batteries can be expensive, so use a calculator with **auto-power-off** or **solar power**, if you can.

Enter your telephone number on your calculator. Press **C**. Now enter a friend's phone number. Press **C**. What does **C** do?

You know that **2 + 3 = 5.** Does your calculator? Try it.

Press **2 + 3 =**

Try other additions . . . it doesn't mind big numbers!
Then try subtractions.

Press **6 − 2 =**

Now try some more.

Sometimes you may get a − in front of an answer. Can you think why this could be? Does it matter which number you put in first?

About your calculator

Most calculators have a **C** button and an **AC** button.
What do you think is the difference between **C** and **AC**?

Try **3** **+** **5** **+** **7** **+** **6** **C** **=**

and then **3** **+** **5** **+** **7** **+** **6** **AC** **=**

Can you work out what happened? If you are still not sure, try

10 **+** **20** **+** **5** **C** **=**

10 **+** **20** **+** **5** **AC** **=**

then

10 **+** **20** **+** **1** **C** **2** **=**

10 **+** **20** **+** **1** **AC** **2** **=**

Clear the display

Keep on pressing **1**. How many figures can you get on your display?

Try out sequences like these

5 **+** **+** **=** **=** **=** etc.

2 **+** **+** **=** **=** **=** etc.

K for constant

Some calculators, not all, have an extra feature.
Try **10** **+** **+** on your calculator. Can you see a
little K on the display?

On some calculators **10** **+** **=** **=** **=** does the same thing as
10 **+** **+** **=** **=** **=**.

You can add 10 to **any** number.

For example, press **10** **+** **+**
(can you see the K ?)

then **8** **=**
then **17** **=**
then **53** **=**

Try out **−** or **×** instead of **+**.

Note to Parents
If your calculator has **C** and **CE** instead of **C** and **AC**, find out what these buttons do with the same sums.

4

☀E for error

Most calculators show you when they can't cope! An E appears on the display. Usually this is when a number is too big for the calculator to handle. Try **1000000 × 1000000** (a million million) on your calculator.

Press **AC** for normal service.

Can you find your own ways to make E appear?

Clever calculator

Your calculator is useful! You can do big sums on your calculator. It doesn't mind big numbers or lots of them!

Can you work out how much all the food in your kitchen cupboard is worth? Guess first.

Let someone else guess as well.

Now use your calculator to add up all the prices. You will need to use the ⊞ button. Remember what you found out about ⊆. Write your answer here.

Either add up the prices again yourself or get someone else to add them up. Is the answer the same?

Note to Parents

Children learn from using a calculator in practical situations. Allow them to add up your shopping as you go round the supermarket!

Your calculator is fun! Find the missing numbers in these sums.

3 ⬜ + ⬜ 6 = 63

50 − 1 ⬜ = 39

21 × ⬜ ⬜ = 273

Write the numbers you found in order in the boxes below.

Numbers					
Letters					

Now look at the code below. When you fill in the right letters for each number you'll find the name of Boffin's friend.

CODE

Numbers	1	2	3	4	5	6	7	8
Letters	S	E	Y	L	D	O	M	I

Draw what you think she looks like.

7

Bull's-eye

Boffin and Cat are playing a game. Cat gives Boffin a mystery sum **?×11=**264 .

To find the answer, Boffin has to guess a number and try it out on her calculator. She tries **30×11=**

Boffin gets 330 . She sees that this is too big.

She tries **25×11=**275 . This is still too big.

So she tries **24×11=**264 . This is a bull's-eye!

Boffin scores **3** because it took her **3** goes to get a bull's-eye.

Now Boffin thinks up a sum ☐ **×20=**260 and Cat has to guess the missing number.

Use these mystery sums to play your own game. Take it in turns to have a go. Count the number of goes you need to have. This is your score. The winner is the one with the lower score.

$\square \times 9 = 126$

$\square \times 13 = 169$

$\square \times 19 = 209$

$\square \times 12 = 192$

$8 \times \square = 224$

$17 \times \square = 289$

Hint

You can improve your score and get very good at this game! These facts will help you.

Even number × even number = even number.

Odd number × even number = even number.

Odd number × odd number = ... number.

Also any number × **5** gives an answer which ends in **0** or in $\square$.

Any number × **10** gives an answer ending in $\square$.

Hex

Use your calculator for this puzzle. Write six 2-figure numbers at the corners of the hexagon like this.

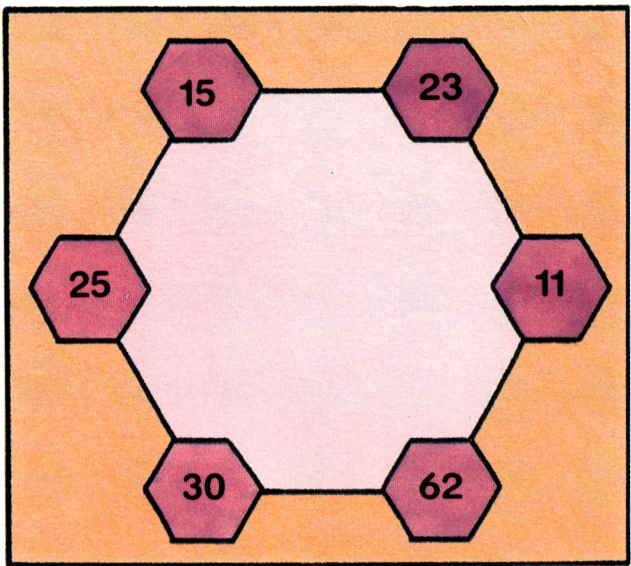

Now go round the hexagon **clockwise** and write down the difference between each pair of numbers.

Write the number **inside** the hexagon if the second number if smaller.

Write the number **outside** the hexagon if the second number if larger.

For example, **23** is larger than **15** so the difference between them, **23 − 15 = 8,** goes on the **outside**.

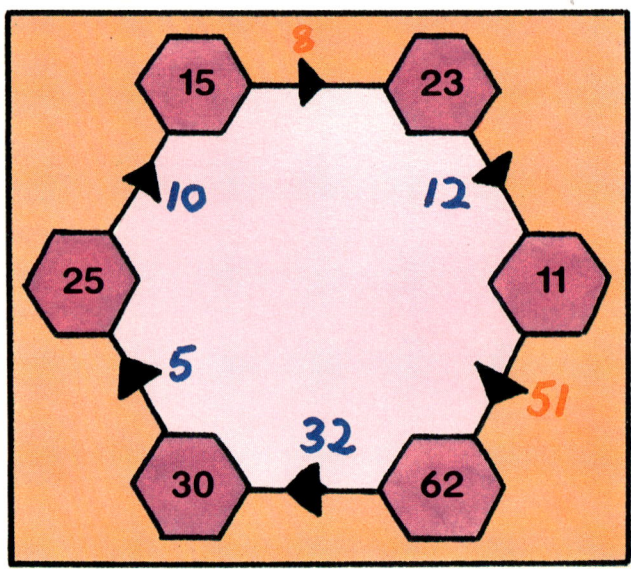

Using your calculator, add the numbers **inside** $5 + 10 + 12 + 32 =$ ▢
add the numbers **outside** $8 + 51 =$ ▢

10

Fill in your own numbers round this hexagon. Does the same thing happen? Now try another set of numbers.

You can even try different shapes! This one is an octagon.

$39 + 9 + 72 + 12 =$ ☐

$33 + 55 + 31 + 13 =$ ☐

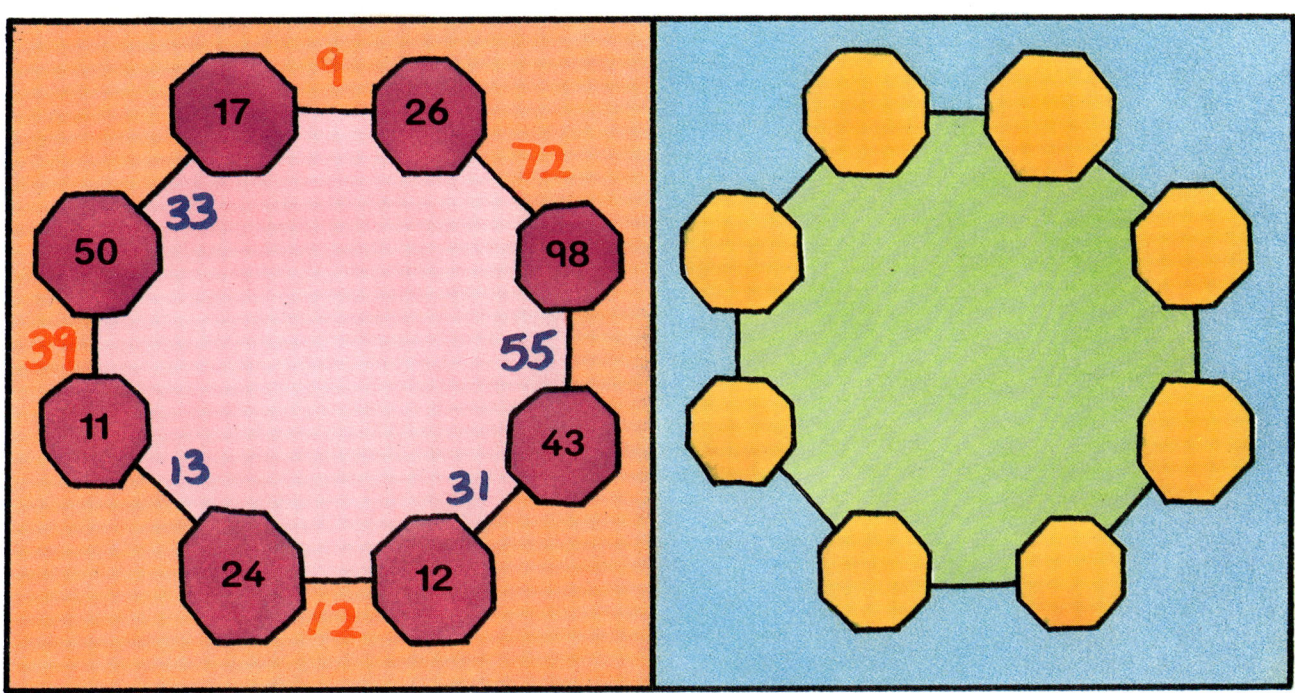

Fill in your own numbers round the other octagon. Does the same thing happen when you add the numbers inside and outside?

Now make up your own shape! Can you think why it works?

11

Magic 22

Take a 3-figure number e.g. **981.** Make all the 2-figure numbers possible out of it.

Hint

There will be six of these. For example, from **981** you can make **98, 89, 91, 19, 81, 18.** Don't choose a **0** or two figures the same in your number.

Estimate what the 2–figure numbers will total [   ]. Then use your calculator to add them.

98 +| **89** +| **91** +| **19** +| **81** +| **18** =| 396

Now add the digits of the original 3-figure number, **981**.

9 +| **8** +| **1** =| 18

Divide your first answer by your second **396** ÷| **18** =| [   ]

Now try a 3-figure number of your own [   ]. Make all the possible 2-figure numbers out of it. Guess what these will add up to [   ]. Now do it on your calculator.

[ ] +| [ ] +| [ ] +| [ ] +| [ ] +| [ ] =| [   ]

Now add the digits of the original number. [ ] +| [ ] +| [ ] =| [   ]

Divide the first answer by the second. [   ] ÷| [   ] =| [   ]

Does this always happen? Try some other numbers to check.

Neighbouring numbers

Boffin gives Cat the number **18**. Cat shows how she can make that number by adding neighbouring numbers. **18 = 3 + 4 + 5 + 6**

Neighbouring numbers are two or more numbers that live next door to each other such as **13** and **14**. Or **6, 7, 8, 9** and **10**.

Now Cat gives Boffin the number **27**. Boffin finds a way to make it from neighbouring numbers on her calculator. She gets
27 = 2 + 3 + 4 + 5 + 6 + 7. But Cat laughs because
27 = 13 + 14 is an easier way to make **27** from neighbouring numbers.

Use your calculator to
1 **Try and make each of the numbers between 1** and **20** from
   neighbouring numbers.
   For example, **9 = 4 + 5** etc.
2 **Find out which 5 numbers between 1** and **20** can't be made from
   neighbouring numbers.

   Can you see a pattern?
3 **Try and make some big** numbers from neighbouring numbers.
   For example, **54, 100, 101, 110** etc.

50

Cat and Boffin are playing a game. Boffin is losing and getting very cross! This is how to play their game.

One person enters **50** on the calculator display. Then you take turns to take away a number under 10 (you can't use 0). The first person to reach **0** wins.

Cat and Boffin's game went like this.

	Cat	Boffin
1st go	**50**	$-9 = 41$
2nd go	$-8 = 33$	$-9 = 24$
3rd go	$-5 = 19$	$-2 = 17$
4th go	$-7 = 10$	$-1 = 9$
5th go	$-9 = 0$ and wins	

Now you can play the game with a friend! After a few games you may see how Cat always manages to beat Boffin. If you get too good, try starting with 100 and taking away numbers under 20.

19

Take any two neighbouring numbers. They can be quite large!

Add them **243** $+$ **244** $=$ 487

add **19** $=$ 506

halve the answer **506** $\div$ **2** $=$ 253

then subtract the first number **253** $-$ **243** $=$ ☐

Try two more neighbouring numbers

☐ $+$ ☐ $=$ ☐

add **19** $=$ ☐

halve the answer ☐ $\div$ **2** $=$ ☐

subtract the first number ☐ $-$ ☐ $=$ ☐

Now try two **enormous** numbers.

For example, **1763** $+$ **1764** $=$ ☐

add **19** $=$ ☐

halve the answer ☐ $\div$ **2** $=$ ☐

subtract the first number ☐ $-$ ☐ $=$ ☐

Do you always get the same answer? Yes No

Can you work out why?

Quite a handful

Using **1, 2, 3, 4** and **5 once** each and the ⊞ button on your calculator, what is the largest number you can make? Is it better to add **523** ⊞ **41** = or **54** ⊞ **321** = or **3** ⊞ **5412** = ?

Try some different possibilities yourself. Here are some spaces for your answers.

Now using the same digits **1, 2, 3, 4** and **5** and the ⊠ button, what is the largest number you can make?

Try **3** ⊠ **5421** = ⬚ and **543** ⊠ **21** = ⬚ .

Try some other possibilities here.

Which of your answers are the largest? Try saying some of them out loud.

How to play

Take it in turns to throw the dice.

Start on **15** and throw the dice to break out of the castle. If the number thrown divides **exactly** into the square which you are on (**15**) move your counter that number forward along the track. If not, stay on the square and try again next turn. Use your calculator to help you. For example, if you throw a 🎲 **15** ➗ **3** = 5 . **3** divides exactly into **15**, so move your counter **3** squares along the track to **14**. But if you throw a 🎲 , **15** ➗ **2** ≡ 7.5 , so you must stay on **15** and try again next go.

Continue around the track like this. The winner is the first player to reach Calculator City.

Calculator Golf

You will need

1 dice
1 calculator
1 pencil

How to play

Decide who goes first.

The first player throws a dice at the start and enters the number thrown on the calculator. The player is then allowed as many shots as he or she needs to reach the next hole. Each shot consists of ⊠ , ⊞ , or ⊟ , followed by a single digit number (1-9) and ⊟ on the calculator. Your score for each hole is the number of shots you take to reach the distance for the hole. You have to cover the distance exactly. Write down how many shots it takes you to cover the distance on the correct place on the chart.

For example, Boffin on hole 1 (target distance 50 metres) throws ⚁

Enter ③ on calculator.

1st shot	③ ⊠ ⑧ ⊟	24
2nd shot	㉔ ⊠ ② ⊟	48
3rd shot	㊽ ⊞ ② ⊟	50

Boffin's score for first hole = **3** because she took **3** goes to reach 50.

The second player throws the dice and plays hole 1. Continue in this way until you have played all the holes. The player with the smallest total is the winner.

START

50m

100m

200m

70m

60m

You can play this game again making your own chart and filling it in.

Hole	Distance	Player 1	Player 2
1	50		
2	100		
3	60		
4	70		
5	200		
6	180		
7	50		
8	80		
9	100		

Remember

millions	thousands	hundreds	tens	units
74,	380,	5	6	1

Seventy-four million, three hundred and eighty thousand, five hundred and sixty-one.

Some of Boffin's relations are very old.
Her great granny is **3658 × 2589** years old.
How old is this? Can you tell someone this number?
Write it in the columns above. Make up your own
big numbers and write those in the columns.

Code name

Sumprod

Boffin chose two secret numbers. She added them to find the sum. 14

She multiplied them to find the product. 33

Then Boffin told Cat the sum and the product. Now Cat has to try to find the two secret numbers using her calculator. Can you help her?

⬜ ⊞ 🟫 ⊟ 14   ⬜ ⊠ 🟫 ⊟ 33

Now you try this game. Choose two numbers. Keep them secret.

Add them.
The sum is ⬜ .

Multiply them.
The product is ⬜ .

Give the sum and the product to a grown up. Ask him or her to use a calculator to discover your secret numbers.

Now the grown up chooses two secret numbers and writes down the

sum ⬜ and the product ⬜ .

Using your calculator, can you find the secret numbers?

18

Divisors

The **digital root** of a number (e.g. **296**) is found by adding its digits (**2 + 9 + 6 = 17**). If the answer has more than one digit, add them again (**1 + 7 = 8**) until you get just one digit. So **8** is the digital root of **296**.

Now use your calculator to find **3** × any number.

Write the answer here.

Find the digital root of the answer.

Now choose five more numbers and multiply them by **3**. Choose some big ones. Find the digital roots of the answers.

Answers					
Digital roots					

What do you notice?

Now can you tell if the year you were born in will divide exactly by **3** **without** using a calculator? Amaze your friends with this trick!

Find **11** × any number on the calculator.

For example, **11** **×** **467** **=** 5137

Find its **alternating** digital root like this

5137 → 5 − 1 + 3 − 7 =

Try **11** × another number and find its alternating digital root.

Now you should be able to tell if a really big number divides by **11**!

Line of four

This is a game for 2 players.

You will need 2 sets of coloured counters or circles of coloured paper.

How to play

Add any pair of these numbers.

2, 3, 8, 10, 14, 20, 51, 67, 99

For example, **3 + 8 = 11**

Put one of your counters on the square that has your answer on it.

101	119	77	102	75	70
24	5	11	18	12	71
107	69	87	13	61	113
23	28	30	10	22	53
118	16	17	59	65	166
54	34	109	150	22	81

Now get your partner to add two of the numbers and cover the right square. Take it in turns. The first player to cover 4 squares with his or her counters in a row in any direction is the winner. For example,

Hint
Use a calculator to help you add!

20

This game is the same except that it uses the × button.

360	30	140	77	35	48
60	110	6	20	200	10
100	75	480	50	300	40
70	22	165	33	30	120
72	15	21	55	220	105
168	150	45	240	14	264

Multiply any pair of these numbers.

2, 3, 5, 7, 10, 11, 15, 20, 24

For example, **2 × 7 = 14**

Cover the square with your answer on it. The first player to cover 4 squares in a row in any direction is the winner.

Can you invent your own game for two players?

Number patterns

Try the following sums on your calculator.

$1 + 2 =$ ☐   now do $2 \times 3 \div 2 =$ ☐

$1 + 2 + 3 =$ ☐   now do $3 \times 4 \div 2 =$ ☐

$1 + 2 + 3 + 4 =$ ☐   now do $4 \times 5 \div 2 =$ ☐

$1 + 2 + 3 + 4 + 5 =$ ☐   now do $5 \times 6 \div 2 =$ ☐

$1 + 2 + 3 + 4 + 5 + 6 =$ ☐   now do $6 \times 7 \div 2 =$ ☐

Can you now find what all the whole numbers up to 100 would add up to without actually doing the sum? ☐

$4 + 85 + 86 + 87 + 88 + 89 + 90 + 91 + 92 + 93 + 94 + 95 + 96$

Now try

$1 + 3 =$ ☐ $2 \times 2 =$ ☐

$1 + 3 + 5 =$ ☐ $3 \times 3 =$ ☐

$1 + 3 + 5 + 7 =$ ☐ $4 \times 4 =$ ☐

$1 + 3 + 5 + 7 + 9 =$ ☐ $5 \times 5 =$ ☐

$1 + 3 + 5 + 7 + 9 + 11 =$ ☐ $6 \times 6 =$ ☐

$1 + 3 + 5 + 7 + 9 + 11 + 13 =$ ☐ $7 \times 7 =$ ☐

Could you now find what $1 + 3 + 5 + 7$ ... all the way up to **99** would be without adding them all up? Follow Cat's hint.

2 is halfway between **1** and **3**

3 is halfway between **1** and **5**

4 is halfway between **1** and **7**

5 is halfway between **1** and **9**

Square numbers

Square numbers are made by multiplying a number by itself.

2 × 2 = ☐   3 × 3 = ☐   4 × 4 = ☐

5 × 5 = ☐   7 × 7 = ☐   11 × 11 = ☐

Can you work out which numbers these are the square of? Use your calculator to try out your ideas.

169

225

289

400

8836

61009

1000000

Criss-cross

Cat puts numbers in each of the yellow squares. Then she adds the numbers across and down and puts them in the green squares.

11 + 13 = 24
8 + 17 = 25

11 + 8 = 19
13 + 17 = 30

Finally she adds the two green squares across the bottom and down the sides.

19 + 30 = 49
24 + 25 = 49

Try your own criss-cross pattern.

What do you notice? Can you see why it works?

What happens if you use a larger grid?

Try the same thing using the ✕ button.

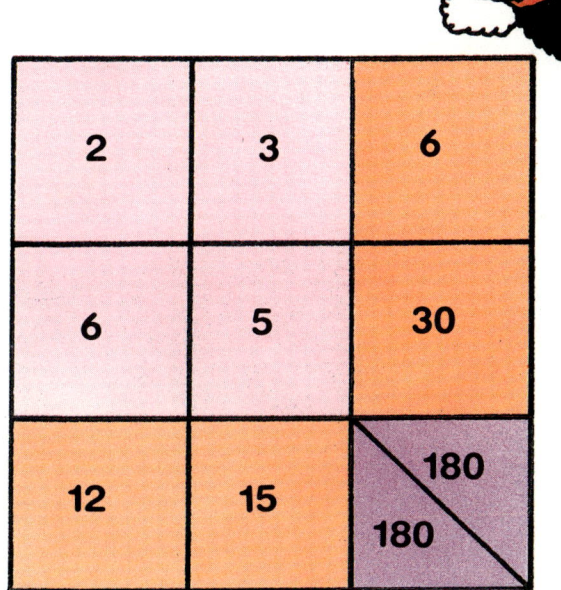

Easy counting

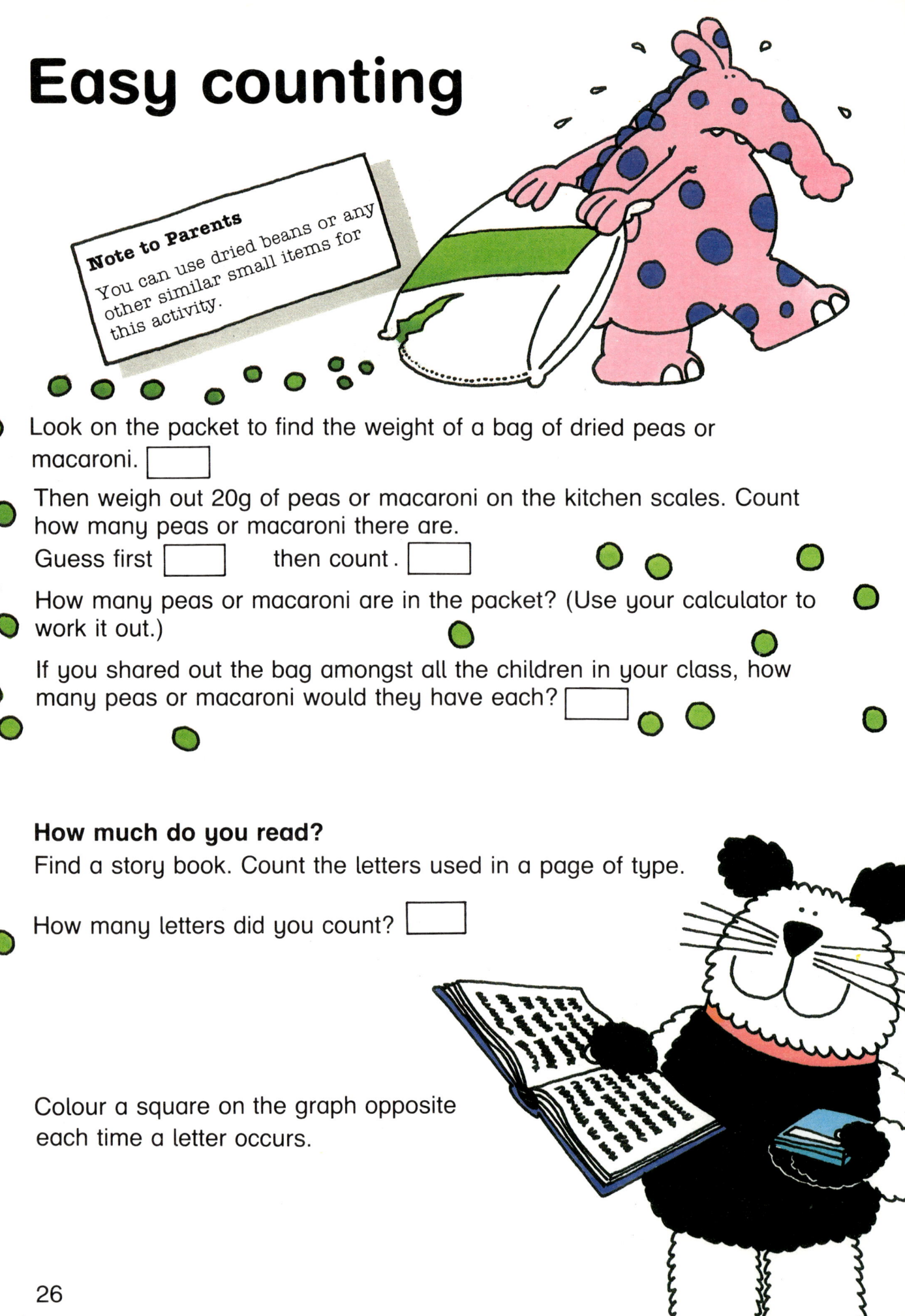

Note to Parents
You can use dried beans or any other similar small items for this activity.

Look on the packet to find the weight of a bag of dried peas or macaroni. ☐

Then weigh out 20g of peas or macaroni on the kitchen scales. Count how many peas or macaroni there are.

Guess first ☐   then count. ☐

How many peas or macaroni are in the packet? (Use your calculator to work it out.)

If you shared out the bag amongst all the children in your class, how many peas or macaroni would they have each? ☐

How much do you read?

Find a story book. Count the letters used in a page of type.

How many letters did you count? ☐

Colour a square on the graph opposite each time a letter occurs.

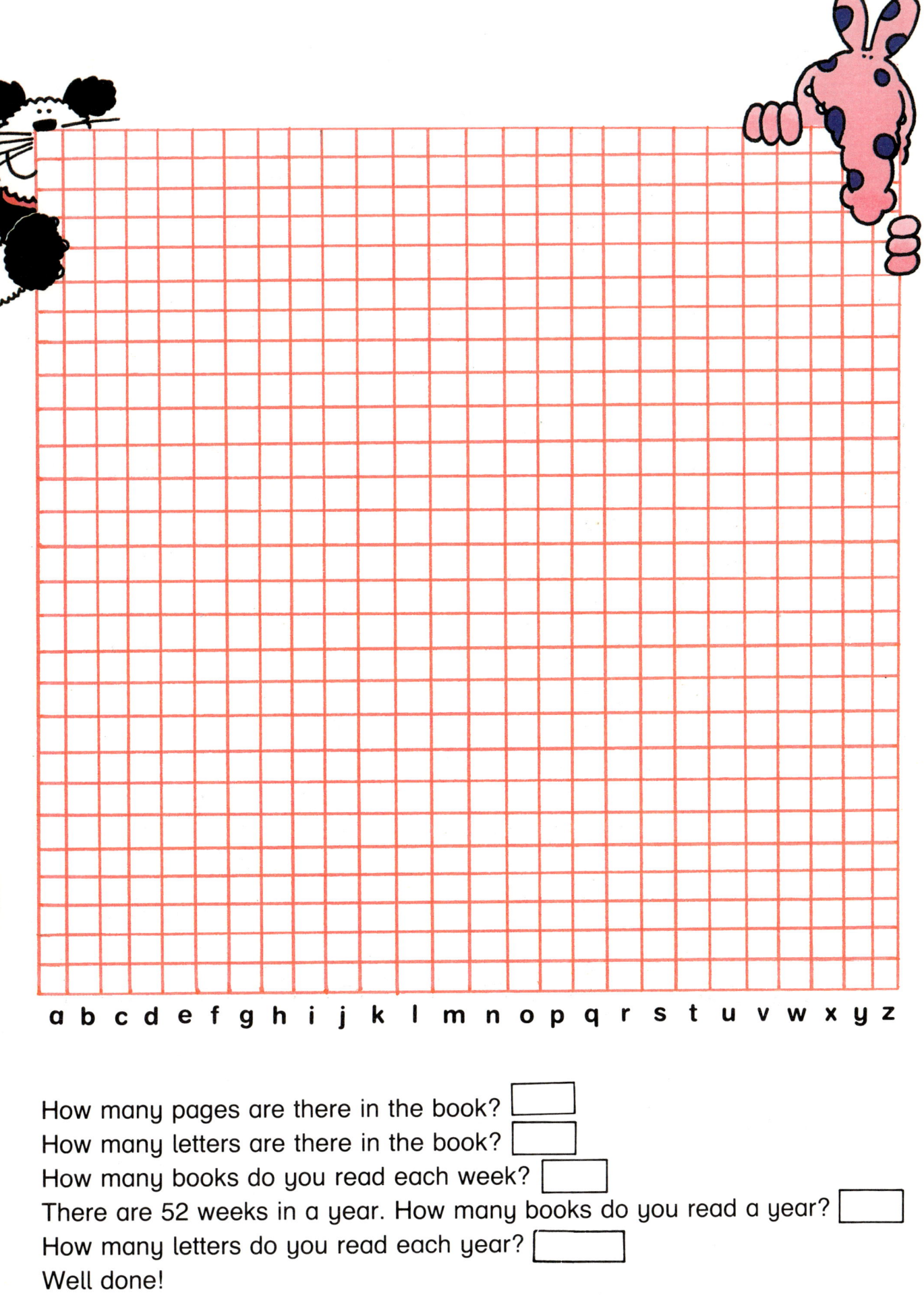

a b c d e f g h i j k l m n o p q r s t u v w x y z

How many pages are there in the book? ☐

How many letters are there in the book? ☐

How many books do you read each week? ☐

There are 52 weeks in a year. How many books do you read a year? ☐

How many letters do you read each year? ☐

Well done!

Big-time numbers

One million minutes?

Use your calculator to find our how many minutes you have been alive.

Remember there are usually 365 days in a year. There are 24 hours in a day and 60 minutes in an hour.

I have been alive [ ] years.

[ ] years is [ ] days.

[ ] days is [ ] hours.

[ ] hours is [ ] minutes.

Altogether I have lived [ ] minutes.

Note to Parents
This will be an approximate calculation rounded down to the number of years old your child is. If you want to do the calculation exactly, you could add on the days in the extra months since your child's last birthday and convert that to days then minutes to add to the total.

Ask your friends to guess how many minutes they've been alive. Then you can work it out for them.

Can you work out how many seconds you have lived? (You may get an E for error, see page 5.)

Take your pulse

To find out how many times your heart beats in a minute, get a grown up to help you take your pulse and count and time it. Write the answer here.

[   ] beats in one minute

Then use your calculator to work out
how many times your heart beats in a hour. [   ]

How many times does your heart beat in a day? [   ]

How many times does your heart beat in a year? [   ]

How many times has your heart beaten since you were born?

[   ]

Point of interest

When you use ÷ on your calculator you may get a number on your display with a little . in it. The number may even fill up the **whole display!**

10 ÷ **7** = 1.4285714

Try **11** ÷ **8** =

One point three seven five.

| Whole number part | decimal point | decimal number part |

Often the decimal part of the number is not important. For example, to share 100 sweets between 7 children do **100** ÷ **7** = 14.285714. The children get about 14 sweets each.

Some decimal numbers can easily be understood as fractions.

Try on your calculator **0.5** ⊞ **0.5** ⊟ ▢

This shows that **0.5** is the same as one half $\frac{1}{2} + \frac{1}{2} = 1$

1 ⊟ **2** ⊟ ▢ also shows that one half = **0.5**.

1 ⊟ **10** ⊟ ▢ shows that one tenth = **0.1**.

3 ⊟ **10** ⊟ ▢ shows that three tenths = **0.3**.

Can you find what decimal number is the same as one quarter $\frac{1}{4}$?

Other decimal numbers are more complicated.

Try one third **1** ⊟ **3** ⊟ ▢

Can you find your own ⊟ sum to fill up the display?

Just for fun, do **3867** ⊟ **5000** and read the answer on the display upside down!

GREETINGS!

31

More about the ideas in this book

This book aims to help both children and parents enjoy working with calculators and understand their uses.

Choosing a calculator for your child

When choosing a calculator the most important things to look for are:

Simplicity: a basic calculator with the usual number operations of $+ - \times$ and $-$, a 'cancel' or 'clear' button **C,** and a memory, is all that is required. A large number of buttons with complex functions is not necessary. Many calculators do have a percentage button **%** , and some have a square root function, but these are not essential by any means. In general, the fewer buttons, the better!

Robustness: a large calculator with strong buttons and which can stand being dropped occasionally is a must for small children. It is important that the buttons are large enough and well enough spaced for children to be able to press them easily and accurately, otherwise unintentional errors can spoil their enjoyment.

Expense: it is not worth paying a lot for a calculator that plays tunes or flashes up messages or pictures. These tend to be nine-day wonders as far as occupying children is concerned, and they also confirm the impression that a calculator is a toy rather than a useful tool.

Make sure that the calculator either has a means of turning itself off automatically, or that the 'on/off' button is both clearly marked and not in a position where the calculator can be turned on by mistake. Automatic 'off' calculators can prove a great saving on batteries, so can solar-powered calculators which do not require any batteries.

What are all those buttons?

Some calculators have more buttons than others — for example several **M** memory buttons — **M+ M− Min MR** etc. It is not necessary to explain or to understand all these buttons in order to let your child experiment. The memory is useful in long additions or complicated calculations. Trial and error is often the best way for a child to discover what function a particular button serves.

Using a calculator

Many parents are dubious about the use of calculators in maths, because they think they may stop children acquiring 'basic skills'. The reverse is in fact true; there are three ways that calculators can be used to further children's mathematical development:

1 A calculator can be used in the same way as other maths equipment, to help children understand mathematical ideas or acquire concepts. Thus, some of the games or activities in this book are designed to help the child understand how 'hundreds, tens and units' work, or how one number fact relates to another.

2 A calculator can help us do a sum which has very difficult numbers in it. The mathematical skill needed here is an awareness of what the answer will look like roughly. It is more important that children realize that 3.8×4.8 is likely to give an answer of a bit less than 20, than that they are able to do a long multiplication sum. The calculator helps with the manipulation of the numbers not the method of doing the sum.

3 Calculators are now a part of everyday life. They are used in many jobs and in higher education. Children who have experience of calculators from an early age are more likely to use them effectively.

It is therefore important that today's children learn calculator skills from the start. This is not to replace 'basic' knowledge but to enable children to handle an accepted feature of modern life with efficiency and confidence.